DANGEROUS LIFE

Also available in the series:

Eve Names the Animals by Susan Donnelly
Rain by William Carpenter
This Body of Silk by Sue Ellen Thompson
Valentino's Hair by Yvonne Sapia
The Holyoke by Frank Gaspar

The Morse Poetry Prize
Edited by Guy Rotella

LUCIA MARIA PERILLO

Dangerous Life

THE 1989 MORSE
POETRY PRIZE
SELECTED AND
INTRODUCED BY
PETER DAVISON

Northeastern University Press
BOSTON

Northeastern University Press

Library of Congress Cataloging in Publication Data

Perillo, Lucia Maria, 1958–

Dangerous life / Lucia Maria Perillo ; selected and introduced
   by Peter Davison
      p. cm.—(The Morse poetry prize ; 1989)
   ISBN 1-55553-059-1 (alk. paper)
   I. Title. II. Series.
PS3566.E69146D36   1989
811'.54—dc20   89-37684
                     CIP

Designed by Ann Twombly

Composed in Weiss by Eastern Typesetting Company, South Windsor, Connecticut. Printed and bound by McNaughton & Gunn, Saline, Michigan. The paper is Glatfelter Offset, an acid-free sheet.

MANUFACTURED IN THE UNITED STATES OF AMERICA
94 93 92 91 90   5 4 3 2

*The poems are dedicated to my teachers—
from whom I've stolen everything. And to
my parents, from whom I did not have to steal
because they gave so much.*

ACKNOWLEDGMENTS

Acknowledgments are due to editors of the following magazines, in which some of the poems first appeared: *Ironwood*: "Firebomber," "Jury Selection," "Collective Invention" (under the title "Movies"), "Deflowering: Three Rites," "Two Parties," and "School." *Ploughshares*: "First Job," "The News (A Manifesto)," and "The Turtle Lovers." *Pequod*: "Landfill" and "Bags."

"The Revelation" appeared in the Chester H. Jones Foundation's *National Poetry Competition Winners 1988*.

"Jury Selection" also appeared in *The Pushcart Prize, XI: Best of the Small Presses*.

The song contained within the poem "Deflowering: Three Rites" is taken from Nayra Attiya's *Khul-Khaal: Five Egyptian Women Tell Their Stories* (Syracuse: Syracuse University Press, 1982), p. 114. Used with permission of the publisher.

Though I have borrowed from both personal and public recollection, the characters and events contained within these poems are in all cases more fictional than real.

Contents

Introduction

Sometimes a moment arrives during the reading of a large quantity of poetry when a poem—if it be in the work of a single poet or in an anthology, or in this case a pile of manuscripts to be judged in a competition—suddenly rises up from its fellows and takes command of the reader's imagination. In my reading for the 1989 Morse Prize such a poem appeared near the beginning of my work: it was "Jury Selection," a poem about a notorious case of multiple rape that occurred in New Bedford, Massachusetts, several years ago at a bar called "Big Dan's."

> She says she only went in for a minute
> to tug on the silver nozzles of the cigarette machine, but
> the thin curtains that line her bedroom windows
> are clearly visible from the street. The whole town knows. Even
> some of these young men
> carry the blue nickels of her thumbprints on the backs of their thighs
> from this time,
> but also the times before. . . .
> We all do violence.

There are better poems, no doubt, in this collection than "Jury Selection," but this one first alerted me to its author's remarkable qualities: a command of imagery (those blue nickels), a true ear for the demotic, a power to rise above the merely autobiographical. *Dangerous Life* impresses me, after many readings, because of its fierce consistency, for the way it will not turn its back on fear, a woman's fear of the violence in her destiny. A thousand tracts excoriating society's addiction to violence cannot equal the chilling effect of these poems: they leave a taste of metal in the mouth. Try "Fire-bomber" or "Photojournalism" or "Diptych: The Milk Carton Children" or "Field Guide to the Dead & Dying Flowers of Eastern North

America" or "The News (A Manifesto)" or "Deflowering: Three Rites."

I know nothing of Lucia Maria Perillo except her poems (though I expect readers of poetry will be hearing more of her). They testify to an Italo-American upbringing with a background in the Bronx but take us on journeys across our continent in search of freedom from the fear that will not vanish: "I kept the merit badge marked *Dangerous Life*, / for which, if you remember, the girls were taken to the woods / and taught the mechanics of fire, / / around which they had us dance with pointed sticks." ("Dangerous Life"). Such fear will not vanish in a present where people play deadly games at parties ("Two Parties") or at work ("First Job") or in the intimacies of female life ("Bags") or in the menace of industrialization ("Cesium: for Goiania, Brazil, September 30, 1987") or in the ways we pursue love ("Logotherapy: After Betrayal" or "Gauntlet").

"Sometimes," Perillo writes, "I feel history slipping from my body / like a guilty bone . . ."; but she insists on keeping track of it, blocking its exit. Her instincts are remarkable for the way they seek out the detail that tells, especially the incident that tells: a young girl swimming in a polluted river, a teenage girl set free, then chastened, by driving too fast, the firebombing (by another teenager) of a gloomy old church and its replacement by a bland new one ("Every month they'd bring / a troop of well-scrubbed teenagers /in yellow suits and dresses, to play guitars and sing *Kum-bay-ya*."), the disturbing lifelong relationship with a brother—and yet she knows the fear of danger for what it is, has the honesty to tell us how it "still gives me a small rush of joy." And there is pride too, justified pride in "enduring, keeping what few secrets lie inside of you / inside of you: heroic myths, ugly rumors— / about God and about some ancient rites of spring."

As you may gather, this book concentrates its attention on the rites of passage that take us out of adolescence into whatever we call its aftermath. Maturity? Adulthood? It happens. We survive. But ultimately the pride evinced in this fascinating and altogether readable volume has less to do with the pride of surviving adoles-

cence than the pride of the poet. Homer has the king of the Phaea-
cians praise Odysseus:

> You speak with art, but your intent is honest.
> The Argive troubles, and your own troubles,
> you told as a poet would, a man who knows the world.

Lucia Maria Perillo, like any good poet, knows the world, and she
speaks with art, reciting the truths and rhythms that have reinforced
her pride:

Some nights I take my lanyards from their shoebox, practice
    baying
those old campsongs to the moon. And remember how they told us
    that a smart girl could find her way out of anywhere, alive.

PETER DAVISON

Ah, my friend, I sometimes think that I
lead a highly dangerous life since I'm
one of those machines that can burst apart!
—Nietzsche

ꜱ꜔ The Sweaters

Used to be, fellows would ask if you were married,
now they just want to know what kind of diseases
you've got. Mother, what did they teach you of the future
in those nun-bred schoolrooms of the sacred heart?

Nobody kept cars in the city. Maybe you'd snuggle
when the subway tunnels ran dark, or take walks
down Castle Hill Avenue, until it ran into the Sound—
the place you called "The End": where, in late summer,

the weeds were rife with burrs, and tomatoes ripened
behind the sheds of the Italians, beside their half-built
skiffs. Out on the water,
bare-legged boys balanced on the gunwales
of those wooden boats, reeling in the silver-bellied fish
that twitched and flickered while the evening dimmed to purple.

What sweater did you wear to keep you from the chill wind
blowing down at the End, that evening you consented
to marry Father? The plain white mohair, or the gray
angora stitched with pearls around the collar?
Or the black cashmere, scoop-necked
and trimmed with gold braid, stored in a box below the bed
to keep it hidden from Grandma? Each one prized,
like a husband, in those lean years during the war.
I see him resting his face against whichever wool it was,
a pearl or a cable of braid imprinting his cheek
while the Sound washed in, crying *again, again.*

Mother, we've abandoned all our treasured things
these days that wear a death-smell in the throat
of each embrace—a death come not by falling to contagion
but by us falling to our knees before those we might have loved
who will kick us and leave us broken. Your sweaters
have long since fallen to the moths of bitter days. And what
will I inherit to soften this hard skin, to make love tender?

3

﹌ Jury Selection

If they only could have put that in the papers, how the winter
    light hangs thickly in those southern Massachusetts towns,
sucking orange at four p.m. from the last spasm of daylight, then
    glowing morbid and humming
with a sound barely audible—not human, more like some rasping
    harmonic/twanged
from the animated hulk of machinery that somewhere keeps it
    all running: this town
where the fish have been abandoned for over a century, the old
    men left
with just the memory of fish swimming in their bones, telling stories
    about the Azores
from their perch on rusted forty-gallon drums that have come to
    rest on the riprap
that's been brought in to seal the village from the sea. And what
    it would feel like to be a man
walking around smothering in the fester of all that—you can
    almost understand why they did it,
raped that woman on the pool table at Big Dan's, in the broad
    daylight of Bobby Darin singing for a quarter
        . . . *now that mackie's back in town* . . .
                and the mown green felt/smelling
of wet wool and—yes sweet jesus—even fish, their blood
    stirring with the sea.
You can almost understand why a woman would have needed it.

But before it gets too complicated, remember: we're supposed
    to work with only the available labels
to construct questions that will discern shades of meaning, measure
    culpability. Whether this woman
has a houseful of gray babies in dirty sleepers, which one's father
    has been named,
where it has happened before, who had drunk which kind of

liquor and how much. She says she only went in for a minute
to tug on the silver nozzles of the cigarette machine, but
    the thin curtains that line her bedroom windows
are clearly visible from the street. The whole town knows. Even
    some of these young men
carry the blue nickels of her thumbprints on the backs of their
    thighs from this time,
but also the times before. Who whimpered, which ones came
    in her
and how often, which ones merely watched without speaking
    from the threshold.

The men were of a darker race, refusing to use our language,
    their dark arms braced
in the ancestral motions of urging we just dimly remember, which
    still arouse us, even in our embarrassment, through the
    electric current
of testimony. Whether a crime has been committed (because the
    woman has her Chesterfields, the change coins clenched &
    sweaty in her palm)
or not, their longboned faces make this offense more palpable—
    the slick skin
and elegant, hard moustaches recalling the brown eyes of our
    own lives, when out of darkness,
the vestiges of an anger we do not claim to know/rise up
    in our bodies
and we seize them and do violence.

We all do violence.

Because the woman was as dark as any of the others,
with no green card and a name you won't find in the phone book.
What is on trial here is a thousand years of women plodding on
    thick legs, their arms draped with string baskets,
toward some market on another continent, where boats pull into

the waiting lips of shore
to meet these women and laud the correctness of their sexless
        march with fruit, and cod,\and men
come home with the musk of Ecuadorian whores still riding their
        loins.
In the end, the real trial takes place in words exchanged
in pissed-up alleyways between tight stone buildings, in words
that are to us guttural and pronounced with too much tongue.
In the end the jury forgives everything but the pool table.
And on the streets of town, in the late afternoon light,
mothers tear their dresses away from stout provincial breasts,
        and carry placards, and weep,
and spit at no one in particular—
for the love of their sons,
not the love of their daughters.

◢❦ The News (A Manifesto)

So today, yet another Guyanan will try to run the border
dressed in a dead housewife's hair—all they've recovered
since her disappearance from a downtown shopping mall.
An "incident," the paper says. Another "routine occurrence"—
wresting my trust ever further from the publicans
assigned to keep us safe, whole. Rather:
vow to stay vigilant against the maiming
that waits hungry in each landscape, even in this
mundane procession of muddy spring days. To see
the tenacity of rooted hair for what it is:
an illusion as fleeting as courage. To keep the meat
between one's ribs from being torn, to keep the hard
marble of the cranium covered with its own skin.
To stay vigilant. To watch for signs of violence stirring
even in one's own machine. To keep both breasts
attached and undiseased. To keep the womb empty;
and yet to keep the organs living there
from shriveling like uneaten fruit, from turning
black and dropping. And not to mistake the danger
for a simple matter of whether or not
to put the body on the streets, of walking
or of staying home—; there are household cleansers
that can scar a woman deeper than a blade
or dum-dum bullets. The kitchen drawers are full of tools
that lie unchaperoned. Even with the doors and windows
bolted, in the safety of my bed, I am haunted by the sound
of him (her, it, them . . . me?) stalking the hallway,
his long tongue primed with Pavlovian drool.
Or him waiting in the urine-soaked garages of this city's
leading department stores, waiting to deliver up the kiss
of a gunshot, the blunted kiss of a simple length of pipe.
But of course I mean a woman's larger fear: the kiss

7

of amputation, the therapeutic kiss of cobalt.
The kiss of a deformed child. Of briefcase efficiency
and the forty-hour workweek. Of the tract home:
the kiss of automatic garage door openers that
despite the dropped eyelid of their descent do nothing
to bar a terror needing no window for entry:
it resides within. And where do we turn for protection
from our selves? My mother, for example, recommends marriage—
to a physician or some other wealthy healer. Of course
it's him, leering from his station behind her shoulder,
who's making her say such things: the witch doctor,
headhunter, the corporate shaman, his scalpel
drawn & ready, my pelt his ticket out.

ꙮ Two Parties

(Montreal, 1976)

Is it just the music that lulls into this somnambulistic
fervor, a swarm of amnesiacs breathing as a single, collapsing
lung? There's a Frenchman in white facepaint flicking a silk
scarf—violet phosphorus under the blacklight—so that it
coils around our limbs like snaketongue. Slender men are
dancing together on the sofa while the Rolling Stones pad
the room with hallucinatory amnion: a midnight specter, black-
cloaked, flinging himself up over the garden wall. And I
embrace him, propelling this neon busload through space with
the frenzied rocking of my hips. Until a speaker squeals loud,
and in a moment of attention I catch the drift of whitenoise
Jagger's been screaming down the floorboards . . .

                                       then the
instrumental break: tortured guitars superimposed like whips
on a woman's falsetto whimpering. *Little girl,* he screams.
Little girl over and over. The mud in my belly rises when I
see the whole room reeling in its stupor, that everyone's long
hair is beating against the sides of their exposed, white
throats . . .

                  and then my friend is in the center of the room
dancing wildly, with next to nothing on. Her body translates
for me why a man might need to knock a girl around sometimes:
the outline of her nipples through her leotard, the gleam of
thigh through the lace tablecloth she's got knotted around
her waist. I clamp my hand hard on her shoulder and whisper
Listen, these girls—; *he's talking about raping and then
strangling them* . . .

                      and then her eyes glaze, the smile she's
been wearing still frozen on her jaw—lips very red and teeth
bared. *I'mma smash out all the plate-glass windows / put my
head through these steel-plated doors.* She knows then the
danger: that we are safe nowhere, not even this room. When

the scarf lashes out at her ankles, they crumple—her legs
splay grotesquely as her knees drop down between them to the
floor, like some inflatable animal I've just knifed. One
thrust, the hiss of air rushing out, then a splatter of
mercury hair on the floor, weeping.

(California, 1981)

My friend had spent the day cleaning up some property on
the dunes along the San Joaquin River. When he returned,
his pickup was full of old bottles and tires and the flotsam
of what people do behind the bushes of deserted places:
condoms, shotgun shells, clothing that's matted hard like
cork. He also brought home an inflatable doll that he found
hanging from a tree, the kind they advertise in the back
of men's magazines. Without seeing it, I insisted that
he re-inflate the thing. We were having a party that night;
I thought everyone would find it funny. Though at first he
seemed repelled by this idea, at my urging he set it up in
the shed behind the house. I watched him drag the tense
form across the patio, clothed in one of his ex-wife's old
housecoats . . .

                  but I didn't get a good look at her until after
the guests arrived. I noticed that some of them wore a pale,
shaken look, that their hands trembled as they moved cigarettes
into their mouths. It was then that I turned to look out the
living-room window and saw her there in the shed, caged by
wire screening. A naked bulb was lit behind her so that her
bright face stood out ghoulishly against the shadows—her
blue eyes large with terror, the bright red lips and inner
mouth molded into a round, dark tube. She was made to be a
child: inflated yellow sausages stood out on either side of
her head, each pigtail topped with a candy-red bow. I thought

then of all the places on her body where my friend might have
had to put his lips so that his breath could enter her, of
him seeing what oozed from her flattened orifices as he hosed
her down against the driveway. And all because I had not been
content to leave her where she'd been put to rest, in a dark
pocket of some stranger's memory, talisman of the horror born
out of unlimited possibility . . .

and because I too had wanted
my turn with her. Knowing that, my skin began to feel the
way hers must have felt: vinyl and static under the shocked
gaze of my guests. I told myself that she was just a thing.
A thing. And that there was no dignity in things.

~~ First Job

Gambelli's waitresses sometimes got down on their knees,
searching for coins dropped into the carpet—
hair coiled stiff, lips coated in that hennaed shade of red,
the banner-color for lives spent in the wake of husbands
dying without pensions, their bodies used in ceaseless
marching toward the kitchen's dim mouth, firm legs
migrating slowly ankleward. From that kitchen doorway,
Frankie Gambelli would sic a booze-eye on them,
his arms flapping in an earthbound pantomime of that
other Frank: The Swooned-Over. "You old cunts,"
he'd mutter. "Why do I put up with you old cunts?"—
never managing to purge his voice's tenor note
of smothered longing. At me—the summer girl—he'd only stare
from between his collapsing red lids, eyes that were empty.

Once I got stiffed on a check when a man jerked crazy-faced
out of his seat, craned around, then bolted
from those subterranean women, sweaty and crippled
in the knees. Though I chased him up the stairs to the street,
the light outside was blinding and I lost the bastard
to that whiteness, and I betrayed myself with tears.
But coming back downstairs my eyes dried on another vision:
I saw that the dusk trapped by the restaurant's plastic greenery
was really some residual light of that brilliance happening
above us on the street. Then for a moment the waitresses
hung frozen in mid-stride, cork trays outstretched
like wide-armed, reeling dancers, the whole
some humming and benevolent machine that knew no past, no
     future—
only balanced glasses, and the good coin in the pocket.
Sinatra was singing "Jealous Lover." All of us were young.

✍ Extraterrestrials

We let the white line drag us down, out of California,
    over the border,
but driving south from San Felipe, we feel sloughing pavement
    about to give out.
And it does—at the El Faro Beach Resort, an ornate RV park
    clutching the dune that is
creeping from under. Mounds of sand slump against concrete
    retaining walls that sprout re-bar
where seams have come loose. A mobile home with satellite
    dish is anchored close
to the beach, the only other tenant an Airstream trailer
    with Iowa plates.

Christmas night, and the bar is open, but dark, cavernous
    and dwarfing three customers:
a Mexican man in a straw cowboy hat, two round brown
    women—his wife and her sister, perhaps.
A big man they call Caesar is tending bar, from the angle
    of the cigarette on his lip,
the peremptory way he stiff-arms the register, we guess
    he's in charge here and say
that we want to park our car at a trailer site, sleep out
    on his decaying beach.
He names a price, we name a price. We haggle. Finally
    he says: *Sleep tonight,*
Talk in the morning . . . two beers his truce. And we stumble
    through muddy Feliz Navidads
before stooping to suck the bottles' cool throats, washing
    the dust from our own.

Maybe it's our presence that snaps them silent: the patrons
    sit frozen mid-slouch,
lost to the green blare of an American movie on cable—
    in English, too lousy for subtitling.

13

A vigilante is dodging cars that skitter on Hollywood
      boulevards: gunning down gas station
attendants and cursing the city through bloodcracked lips.
      The camera cuts—
to a hooker named Princess, a tired blonde girl whose lips
      lag behind whatever she's saying,
as though she were divorcing herself from the vacuous words
      her mouth must release.
One of the women occasionally breaks her stare at the screen
      to fret after some children
outside. On a square of plastic turf, two well-freckled boys
      run frenzied and white as phosphor
through a gauntlet of chattering local kids who're clobbering
      heads with long-handled nets
once used to clean the pool. The pool is empty now, cracked
      and full of sand and the palm fronds that shaded
the sunken poolside grill unravel and hiss against each other
      in the charged night wind. Meanwhile:

Princess has landed in bed with the vigilante, both of them
      naked & oily & barking, though the girl
will not look at the camera. Their skin sets off a tremor
      in the women—the wives or the sisters—
as though they've recognized something they smell in the room.
      And slowly they turn
to look me over, eyes settling on my sneaker's ruptured toe
      before flickering
to the graying man beside me: not enough likeness for father,
      or brother, his hand
absently stroking the back of my neck as we watch our bodies
      from another country:
the girl without belly or child, the man with the gun
      and the wallet.
But already the vigilante has jumped in a cab with a fistful
      of Princess's money.

Keep the change! he calls to palm trees while speeding away,
    as though they could hear.
But the man in the cowboy hat—husband or brother—has heard,
    and convulses with laughter.
KEEP THE CHANGE! he cries out, chuckling: *he! he! he!*
    And then silently, into his beer,
he moves his lips over and over again with these words,
    as if to fix against loss
the message he's received from a world beyond, passwords
    he'll use to salute its citizens
when they arrive with their machinery ablaze to deliver him,
    deliver him like a pizza
to the doorstep of a ranchstyle home and lawn whose thirst
    is always watered green.

Later: we drop clothes in a pile, stand naked on the beach
    with a sleeping bag flapping
between us. We settle it down on the sand, and set down
    our faulty bodies,
then the remaining bag on top. My right hip juts
    chilly to the breeze but I don't draw closer,
oh no, to the man beside me—fearing those greasy half-nelsons
    fleshed out by our doubles on the screen.
On Cortez's sea, green lights head north: the fishing boats
    we saw this morning, Christmas morning,
loading their ragged crews of barefoot boys in San Felipe.
    And now, the holy day gone,
I imagine their splintered feet, the salt chill in their spines.
    When I squint hard at Orion, the stars wax
just perceptibly bigger, as though falling slowly to Earth.
    I elbow the man from his sleep
just to let him know I know how they'll arrive: spaceships
    will trundle from the sky
as silver trailers in a relentless stream of border traffic,
    dirtbikes, speedboats for their comet-tail,

and bearing deliverance for those who've prepared the words
    to greet them—
                     Sleep tonight,
he says, putting a hand out to still me. *Talk in the morning.*
    But by morning, those
who sleep the beach have sometimes vanished from the sand—
    are we to be among the taken?
From far off, I hear children shriek in mongrel tongues . . .
    half the takers, half the taken.

✻ Deflowering: Three Rites

In Cairo, the heaviest aunt will pin the girl's arms
above her head and knead her thighs open.
The girl is maybe twelve, has always rejoiced
in the firm muscle torquing between her legs
when she races against her brothers in the alley,
filling her body with speed, a body
that would be otherwise small.
But now she *is* small, watching her groom
wind the white gauze around the fat gold rings
on his first two fingers. Throwing a pair of silver anklets
beside her on the cot, he lunges forward
with one hand mummied stiff, while outside the door
the women sing

> *Did you whiten the gauze, O Bride?*
> *Your husband is a joker, O Bride.*

And then his strange fingers are inside her,
breaking the seam of skin
that held her shut. There is pain, yes,
but the scream is stopped in her throat
by the woman's thick hand, reaching down
to clap her jaw tight. The man pulls his fingers
out, smiles when he sees the gauze splashed
with the petals of a rusty flower. Satisfied,
the company leaves the girl to heal herself
and goes out singing her blood in the streets

> *On an aluminum bed, whether you cry or not*
> *This is a night worth the world!*
>
> *On a bed made of brass, whether you cry or not,*
> *Consider it a night among nights;*
> *It will soon be over.*

17

She passes the night with her knees tucked fetal,
under her chin, while the gauze is passed
among uncles and cousins, men who—
because they cannot have her—avenge themselves
by this taking-back of the blood
that causes their denial. Her hands
clench and unclench in the dark, waiting
for his return. It will soon be over.

*　　*　　*

This morning's paper, in Managua:
the man is teaching the women how to load clips
into a Soviet-made AK47 automatic rifle.
The backdrop appears to be some gutted schoolroom—
crayoned fuselage is posted on walls
that dissolve into the dotted oblivion of the laserphoto.
The three women are leaning in toward him, wide-eyed
and yet amused, their smudged gray faces almost smiling.
One of them is still unrippled in the chest—
a girl. (He would need
to have himself a girl.)
He is holding the clip in his hand,
out in front of his face like a microphone
and his mouth is open
with a word. He is telling the women
not to regret the parting of their innocence,
but he tells it in a legend of their people,
a parable about the woman who wove
baskets out of husks
she gathered from the jungle floor.
And it begins:

> *Just as the papaya drops its pale petals*
> *before the coming of the rains . . .*

*　　*　　*

She was a chubby girl, a sixth grade classmate
who took me up to her attic and took off her clothes
and lay down on the floor and cranked her knees up
to her chest, and spread her legs apart. She kept her toes
very pointed, like a ballerina, a position
she'd perfected from a grainy photo
in some medical book—*even your parents do it this way*,
she said. Her strong legs were able to hold the pose
for a long time in the failing blue light
between school and supper, as she defined for me
the particular innuendo of each crook
in her limbs. And I remember my amazement,
how it did not seem possible that either of us
could support the weight of our father's body
in the precarious fulcrum of those flexed knees.
More than half my visions were shattered there, by the raft
of her exposed white nakedness, those peculiar arched
toes I never came to understand, the gray
and paleflowered panties hanging off her left ankle . . .
I could see every hair on her stomach raised in preparation
for the moment they'd be met by another belly
on this dusty floor. She already had small bosoms.
Closing my eyes on her, I sought that moment but could find
my body as nothing other than alone, locked forever
in her stiff white tetany. I had no bosoms,
would make no preparations, determined
no desire would force my turgid surrender
of that uninhabitable body:
Poised. Graceful. And unready.

For the Catholic Girl

These days your thoughts turn to what must be done
these days, to get the knives back in the blood.
When you were young/it was easy: night wore
the blue smell of light rain on the pavement,
and you'd steal your father's German car
and go riding, alone, on the parkway: two-lane road
with a three-inch clearance between the guardrail
and its reflection streaming across the doorhandle.
You follow the stink of the Bronx River up
to where the eyes of roadside animals come fast,
then faster. Zooming by flat weeds marking their paths.
Around fifty-five you turn the radio up to drown
black banners' slapping against the windshield:
darkness slips its tongue inside your mouth
while your back teeth grind themselves to emery.
Punching sixty-six, then seven . . . your arms rod-stiff,
virginity pitched in a heap out on the road.
Until somewhere well into the upper double digits,
your eyes fixed beyond the stadium wall of the high
beams' arc, Sister Joseph Anastasia starts pounding
her righteous measuring rule against your skull,
and your tongue routs one of its classroom amnesias:
Though I'm racing my ass through the shadow of some god
damned valley I fear . . . blah blah, blah blah . . . no death . . .

But there your engine starts to choke and quit—
don't get me wrong, the car was running good.
Just your nerve failing when, this time like always,
that stupid riddle rams itself into your heart:
If a dagger travels halfway to its target every second,
when does it ever make its mark? And you
were the lady whirling for the carnival knifeman;

you were Mrs. William Alfred Tell.
Waiting for a strike that never came, that test of days
when every notch on the speedometer was just a measure
of how far you were from where you'd never be.
Until gravity eased you into the lefthand shoulder
where you pulled a U-ie in the ditch where only cops
were supposed to go. Then downstream, headed back
into the shadow of the valley that led you home.
Where you lived in the shadow of algebra homework due.
The valley of explanations. You hadn't been changed a bit.
Jesus fucking H: you were still a fat girl,
with dirty hair and not a single dagger through your heart.

✺ Bags

They brought the sixth-grader girls to the middle school's attic
    where we sat under the dull yellow eyes
of the *shim* parked dusty in the corner: anatomical model
    half man, half woman, the torso's
breasted half cut away to reveal female organs underneath.
    Strains of a high-pitched yelping
drifted up from outside, where the boys pummeled themselves
    against each other in the dirt.
But we held steady as small nuns, there in the purple half-
    dark, pronouncing the dark
unpronounceable words until the school nurse said: *This*
    is what makes you a woman, raising up
the sanitary pad by one of its tails as though it were
    a dead white weasel
she'd found by the side of the road. Her hand trembled.
    And I knew I was nothing like a woman.

But when I first found the darkness spreading inside my own
    underwear, I thought of the dead thing.
And told my sister who told my mother who gave my sister to
    give to me: a flesh-colored plastic bag
to put the bloody dressings in. All the other weapons—
    the pink box and foil packages—
were easily explained, but the bag, slippery and new as a
    fish . . . Nobody told me
how I'd know when I was through with it, or how the bag
    was to be disposed.
Like a chalice, or the flag, I knew it could not be destroyed
    in the conventional ways.
So I hid it in my closet, where it grew as though infected—
    I collected more bags—
my damp & inner-body smell suffusing the room so thickly
    that I soon felt as though I were living

inside the wet bowels of a transfiguring creature who was
        half me and half some new
strange thing. And I wore that bigger body around on me
        everywhere, because my clothes all stank.

I had to be almost a year older before I got enough courage
        to risk sneaking the bags
into our galvanized trash cans, buried under some newspapers
        and gutted fish remains from last
night's supper, where I'd hoped nobody would stumble onto them
        and discover my betrayal,
the awful way I'd broken the unspoken regulations. Even now,
        telling you this,
I am somewhere giving myself demerits. Because what the school
        nurse held was not a weapon
but a gag; silence the tacit vow surrendered there under
        the attic's yellow eyes:
DOMINE ECCE SIGNUM INTERDICTUM: the small voodoo we
        learned never to leave perched on a
bathroom radiator, bodily flotsam to be taken to the soul
        and chambered there, surfacing
only as the filtered odor of familiar decay, maybe only
        a feminine cast to the skin
our mannered acquaintances will pretend to ignore, their gaze
        drifting back and again back
to the anomaly's source, the way eyes won't be staved off
        the sixth finger on a hand. And she grows
less discrete each day, despite my attempts at rendering her
        transparent: that bigger woman
I still wear on my masculine spine like an old rubber raincoat
        grown moldy from seasons of use—
yet unwilling to be loosed, trashed, shook free.

Jimi Hendrix and Phyllis Iannotta
Speak Out against the Agenda

"We have to locate ourselves on the boundaries,
which cannot be done by following yesterday's
ideas, but by setting our own intellectual agenda . . ."

—*Memorandum, Syracuse University English Department*

Today in the Sunday *Times*, a book reviewed about the famous
    murder of a Manhattan bag lady.
Some journalist has woven for her a history—born on a steamer
    bound from Italy to Ellis Island,
the first half of her life spent dancing at the Rosedale, playing
    gin rummy, filling the blanks of crosswords
with unflinching zeal. Then the rest—how she came to stop
    working, then bathing,

soon an offense to her friends. How she began setting fires and
    stuffing whole rolls of toilet paper
down public johns. About her stays in flophouses and clean-up
    tanks run by the sisters of mercy
who watched her labor over her precious crosswords while the
    blanks grew clotted with words
having no referent beyond her own mind, anagrams of her refusal
    to comply with the rules of the game.

On Sundays I walk to the drugstore for the heavy paper—not just
    for the pretense of absent funnies,
more for a routine that'll help me hang on. If I go a few days
    without taking a shower, the panic
sets in: *Is this it? The descent? Now?* I begin surveillance of my hands
    for other ways they might lapse—
shoplifting small & useless items, say, or adopting the habit of
    covering my teeth when I speak,

until a bowl of Campbell's spills over on my only set of sheets
    and I am grateful
for an excuse to fall back into old routines: to watch the laundry
    spin, and shop for eggs.
I won't pretend these things are easy, but when they are done
    I can look at my day and tell myself
that life has not been wasted, that the machinery still hums
    gladly for a few boundaries intact.

But years ago I remember seeing Hendrix on *The Tonight Show*:
    Carson was trying to make him speak,
but he wouldn't or couldn't, and so, having to be led a little,
    was asked to tell sixty million Americans
about his day: *You get up and . . . ?* The musician just stared,
    his upper lip scattered with stray black hairs
and curling back like a dog's when he said: *Yeah I try and get up
    every day . . .*

But look what these people had coming: one of them choking
    to death on his puke,
the other one sliced in a parking garage on West 40th Street—
    both as though slain by some arm
of the law that's been trained to coerce our toes to the line,
    or else break them.
And we collect the newsclippings as fuel for the twin furnaces of
    our own repentance and compliance.

Today the house is too cold for bathing/and the laundry calls
    for quarters that evade me
and the refrigerator seethes with rotten food. But tomorrow
    I'll rise early and tick items off a list.
Tomorrow. I've read that birds who live near offices build nests
    out of staples and paperclips when they can't find
grass or twigs: that ancient voice in their hollow bones, twisting
    the arm of habit.

✦ His Wife Goes Walking

Closing the door on rank yellow light from
his warm & slipperfooted house, I step out
into the night, wet as the mouth of a large
black dog. I choose a street with the hope
that it leads to this beast's black heart,
whose black drums mount in the back of my
throat. At the top of a hill with the city
glistening below, there's an alley into which
I turn. The concrete walls on either side
are tall and so long they appear to converge.
Ahead, another woman has entered, her footfall
made deafening by the slim corridor. I follow
the spiked shadow of her frail body, backlit
by a swath of orange vapor, the city's breath,
that lies far off, past the end of the alley.
I let my heavy footsteps fall in behind her.
She hurries her pace, never turning around.
I walk faster, closing the space between us.
How easy it would be now, to run and knock her
down! I work hard to keep from playing games
with my feet: rapping out a fast staccato
rhythm, slapping the pace of an erratic jog.
The woman shifts nervously from wall to wall.
I let my right leg drag behind me, the left
stepping hard, sounding the irregular hiss
and tock of a limping madman. I tuck my hair
in my hood, cover my chest with my muffler.
When she turns, I keep my head low, watching
through the ragged wool of my bangs until
I see it, yes, her fearful white eyeshine—
like that of a deer caught in the headlights
of an onrushing car. Her hair falls away
from her throat as she turns forward again,

her raincoat hem swaying against the back of
her calves. She breaks into a trot then breaks
into the orange gases of the night at large.
I have let her go because a god is merciful/
once He is assured that all poor animals
are toys to his will. As *he* is assured—
each night he sees me bent over the ironing,
or bent over the poor animals we have made.
But for a moment it was I who might have made
her head bleed; I might have made her utter
the word *please*. I walk home with a stick
and a monkey's grin. My husband still sits
in his chair by the fire, as though nothing
has changed. When he asks how the night was
I say: Like an animal with warm breath,
and smile as I go about his small chores.
Because I can look at my hands and know
they are not the same hands I set out with.

ᶴᵉ Posterity

I have pictures of my girlfriends' babies
lined across my windowsill like a deck
of pornographic playing cards; the flesh
is all the same, but the positions vary.
Night & day, they gaggle
until the felt-tip writing on the back
comes bleeding through their clear blue eyes,
each happy, open mouth as black and wet
as my insides are dry: this wildwest diorama
where taut pink hides crawl bloodlessly
across a landscape pocked with thorns.
Ah, the flesh that looks so soft, so weak,
is as impervious as tungsten, and as sure,
and as surely bent on commandeering my own face
as were the pods replicating smalltown citizenry
in *The Invasion of the Body Snatchers*.
Which is what they are, aren't they—
body snatchers?
Is this where all my old girlfriends
have gone to? To the land where the zombies are
our children, secretly incubating the various
postures of our hands they will need
to move among us unnoticed? And we tell ourselves
that this is nothing, nothing at all, to fear?

✍ Collective Invention

When I was a kid, my brothers and I went to movie houses
to watch Moe poke the other Stooges in the face, and the men
in padded suits shimmy their hands through the air,
loose as two twitching fish, then that sound—
va-va-va-voooom: the torso of a woman
sketched sexy as an hourglass, with a narrowing in the middle
we knew was the important part, where the babies dropped out.
We never paid attention to her head or feet.
And so there is something rather frightening
in the way you would now so willingly pour yourself in through me
because you are done with yourself and want to rest.
You give the same reason for wanting to have this child
my father gave—about the good genes, though four kids were too
    many
for my mother, who never bought a ticket for the show. She only
    drove.

There is a picture by Magritte of a mermaid, but inverted.
she has legs with toes and her head is a fish.
This is the sort of experiment I want to perform on you and me
so that we could switch places, and I would have the power
to put my own ashes—which are not cold yet, nor dead—into the
    urn
at the bit of your belly, the vestigial place of birth.
And with them you could make any kind of monster you wanted
    out of me—
skewed eyelids resting on that white, translucent skin, a kid
with flippers where the arms are supposed to be.
This could be your little brother Curly, whom you maim daily,
who still loves you. Who trusts your murderous eyes
if only because they remind him of his own. In the grainy & flickering
    darkness,

the leather seat gulps me like a draught of air, and I keep my hands
        between
my older brother's knees to stave off menace from the father
who my father has put inside of me. His presence is as real as the
        finger
moving stiff-jointed and straight, into my eye. & the sound it makes
on implosion: *tock*. There is not enough trust in this world for me
        to buy it—
the stunt men, the feigning—not among fathers
or brothers, not between lovers.

Cesium: For Goiania, Brazil, September 30, 1987

> How can this infinite beauty and sovereign glow
> Fail to burn even as I am burning?
>
> —Michelangelo Buonarroti

Take the example of the young Buonarroti,
who sees in his marble quarried from Carrara
no beauty in this world the stones might not contain:
this one the voluptuous, stopped climax
of the slave who surrenders to his death in sexual release,
that one the proud bastard de Medici and all his ducats,
and the slab of pinkish opalescence, squarely cut . . .
dare he be so blunt to claim that one is God?
Likewise, the scrap metal dealer earns his keep
by gauging not the surface nor the mere appearance of a thing—
for a copper pipe is lighter than a lead one,
and silver grows more oxidized than steel.
So when he finds the concrete lozenge on the junk heap,
he knows better than to simply pass it by.
Weighing more than three of him, the gray oblong
is carted to his house in a borrowed wheelbarrow.
He drags an old brown rug out to the yard, and for hours
sweats with chisel, never raising question to the work.
Finally, he makes his best strike with the sledge:
the egg splits—and sun pours out!
A gold so shiny that it hurts your eyes!

It spills like chalk: in lumps and dust.
In the holy, other-worldliness of its metallic sheen,
the scrap metal dealer feels himself almost a saint.
Children come running, and plaster the yellow dust
to their faces and throats, as the day decays
in a sunset paling against their hoard of light,
yet marking time that soon will bring

31

the nausea, and the endless burning of their skin.
But before it's too late, go back again—

Take the example of the agèd Buonarroti,
who finds nine-tenths of beauty not to be salvation,
but retribution: he can make Christ die
and die again, but never in these stones shall He be risen.
He carves more slaves but leaves the heads and hands and feet
still buried deep inside of rough-hewn blocks.
And the scrotum that was once the sculptor's pride
is left a raw, undifferentiated mass.
Only the rack of each torso is carved
true enough, the muscles webbing in each chest
so that the figures seem to convulse and strain
against bearing their own suffering to this world.

Call this the non-finito: this recognition
that the world encases forms best not brought forth,
no matter what their brilliance. In Goiania,
people gild their bodies with what they believe
to be the earth's good gift, an earth that they
devour in Communion: *This is my body, eat of me*,
though the half-lives they are eating are in truth their own.
The children run home to sleep with glossy bodies—
for a time they are golden, ethereal.
And even the scrap dealer can't help but take a lump
to bed with him like the wife he does not have.
All night the isotope spins in his palms like the globe of God.
All night he bathes in its phosphorescence.
In his dreams he wanders through the halls of great museums.
But when the sun crawls over the horizon,
it ignites his skin, and the monuments he's dreaming.
The great works burn in the flames of their own artistry.
And history now grieves us, for we've found
that artistry a lie and all the dead masters wrong:
Beauty alone will never save us.

Logotherapy: After Betrayal

that I ran into my friend Vic was a good thing
because we leaned on the shadowy cars and he gave me
some new words: Faith, Reconciliation, Continuance.
But driving home, they began to fill me up with grief
so I tossed them out the window like a finished cigarette.

And I went down to talk to the creek, who was filled with a grief
of her own, a grief of too much water having fallen
in too few days. And she had me dash my empty beer bottles
against her tortured stones that night, had me make
the shrill cry of a hawk as I let each one fly.
And with each crash she gave me back my former words,
my old & tarnished words, the *f*s and *t*s
honed sharp enough to really hurt somebody bad. And sharp
enough to hack a trench into my chest, so the water could roll in
like freshened blood, roaring the way it roars against
the creekstones: *girl you're alive, alive, alive* . . .

I call the creek a woman because she had a woman's wisdom,
a woman's bitter tears, even had the housewife's old cliché
about how all love ends in either death, or separation
from those we love. And the creek made me remember
how they want you to believe your only way off the meathook
is by dying first.
She said: whatever you do, whatever you do
don't let yourself be the one who dies first.

✎ School

for Jacques Lacan

At four in the afternoon, outside this classroom, there's a world
    turning blue
and thick as chalk. But the windows have been built small, so as
    not to snag one's attention
with the garbled love of pigeons, or the construction machines
    gnawing on the carcass
of an indigent street below. The man at the lectern is sweating,
    his young face worn with postulation
in these moments that ascend to his unveiling of all the old
    fictions: that what we used to believe
was the body moving through instinctive blunders of passion, heart-
    ache, has all the while
been nothing more than a shaft of light traversing a dusty room,
    that the labels *you* and *I*
are walls we've erected to house the criminally insane . . . etc.,
    etc. . . . —in short, that we are only
the sum of what's been done to us.
I don't know.
Maybe I don't have it quite right.
One pigeon/and I lose the thread of his entire argument, which
    dribbles away in particular words
like *language* and *unconscious*. Until the man falls to his seat—
    grown suddenly, overpoweringly
spent. And for a moment I catch in his face the boy even he
    once was, holding his head in his hands,
air-starved. Beneath the translucent skin at his temples, I watch
    the veins on his skull growing large.

*

Truth is, what I remember of my childhood is little of my
    mother, less of my father—

a few friends, perhaps, but mostly a bike that still haunts me:
    a Raleigh three-speed,
painted gold, with handbrakes—having newly fledged the safety
    of the coaster brake, the training wheel.
Blue afternoons I'd ride her into the maw of likely collision—
    sometimes, I'll admit,
plagued by the deeper questions of being:/ because my house
    butted up against the schoolyard;
did that make me different, somehow inverted, from the other
    children who only knew its tortures
by day? And what had carving my initials in the schoolyard
    beech done for my mortality?
Next door lived two German girls whose mother rinsed their hair
    in olive oil, who spoke
a glottal language that I chanted back at them. My mother was
    nothing more than a small disruption,
one that could be placated with a gift of wild mint or a good
    grade in spelling, from whom
I could pinch all the small necessities: matches, kitchen knives,
    jelly sandwiches.

But the schoolyard was a bigger universe than anyone could
    exhaust—it did not have boundaries,
the way a school seems bounded, invariably, to me now. There
    was a cinderblock retaining wall out back,
set into a hillside overlooking the Half Moon Apartments, on the
    walltop some high spikey grass where we'd lie
with our bikes stashed, invisible to the apartments below. The
    German girls once took me to visit
an aunt who lived there—I remember finding the buildings so fly-
    specked and public: the front door
that was never completely your door, the walls your father'd
    heave the kitchen chairs against,
never wholly his walls. The aunt had arthritis bad enough to keep
    her fingers stiff and her

in a wheelchair, and a bowlfaced Aryan son who wheeled her in
     the halls.
But their window was not *the* window, dead-on from where we'd
     hide in the weeds.
In that window—always? almost always?—we'd find the torso of a
     man from shoulder to mid-thigh, naked
and surreally white against the interior of a dim room, as though
     we were looking outward
through the panes, on the trunk of a smooth white tree. Gauze
     curtains blew from the window frame, swaying
the same way the man would sway and tremble until his whole
     body went rigid, then suddenly left the window.

It seems odd now that I don't remember his penis, but perhaps
I had not yet learned to attach importance to one part of the
     body over another. So much for Freud.
It has taken me this long to admit I don't really care what makes
     us the way we are, that it seems pointless to care
when outside this classroom window there are Indians dancing
     across the girders of a highrise going up
at ten below. Why did we stop going to watch the naked man?
     Did we start, so early, to busy ourselves
over boys? Or get scared—because we could feel ourselves
     falling, falling to the magnetic fields
of their alien bodies? In my mind I keep some footage of a small
     boy leaning out the window,
yelling at us to go away, quit spying on his dad—but this clings
     without proof, and I prefer to believe
we went unnoticed, even though, years later, my mother told me
     stories from the last days of the old
Half Moon, before they sold it off as condos: *Such a better class*
     of people now, and someone made a pretty penny . . .
She told me how the son was to find his crippled mother lying
     motionless on the bathroom tile—
almost forgetting to mention how someone finally had the good
     sense to call the cops on Mr. H. before

he did God-Knows-What to every little kid in the neighborhood.
Still I prefer to believe
I went unnoticed, that I was the hunter, not the hunted, that
    maybe the village justice had misunderstood
what we were learning from Mr. H.'s guiltless flesh. This pale
    rider would never have allowed herself
to be "done to." I keep my own body under wraps now, try to
    keep my knees beneath the table during lectures,
keep the tongue from wagging out of my mouth: *Epistemology,*
    phooey—a steelworker knows what he knows.
Each lull in the classroom brings another stupid thing I could say
    out loud.
I've bought an old bike, with a coaster, that I use
    to get around campus—
and yes, the rear wheel banging down off the curb, under my
    weight, still gives me a small rush of joy.

✒ Paradise Raceway

At Paradise Raceway, the horses run in circles round the grass
for my old man. Sunday, he's taking his best girl to the track,
warning her: *just don't let anyone look up your dress.*

We're riding in his fancy car, a Cadillac express
—my father rides up front, I'm lying down in back—
next stop Paradise: horses running circles around the grass.

All the dirty people in the grandstand watch us
through a fence. While the uphill escalators rattle-clack,
I'm looking pretty careful at who's looking up my dress.

They got tablecloths in the clubhouse; one wall's glass.
They got T.V.s showing horses being groomed out back,
thinking this is Paradise, their muzzles circling in the grass.

A man swaggers to our table. *Boy you'd be better off at Mass,*
he says, and gives my father's cheek a little whack.
(I try to look mature and fold my hands up in my dress.)

They leave me sitting there, but my father comes back fast,
stuffing twenty-dollar tickets in the pockets of his jacket,
just in time to watch the horses run, circling the grass.

He bet on the seven horse, screams when he sees it finish last:
YOU LARD-ASSED WHORE! And when he's caught my legs
    sprawled slack—
*GODDAMMIT LOU, I TOLDJA EVERYONE'D BE LOOKING UP
    YOUR DRESS!*
And our own running home is ragged, as though that Cadillac
    were lurching desperate circles around Paradise's grass.

❧ The Turtle Lovers

Those armored domes would appear at random,
the gifts of chance. Like us hearing the sinister
rustle of leaves during a stalled moment
of those games we played in the woodlot.
My little brother and I
would bring the box turtle home, where we'd built
a cage out of old window screens. At first
it'd clap shut if we prodded
the withered skin lining its neck and limbs—
but soon it lost fear.
When we'd raise the beast by its battered hull
the leathered arms and legs would flail, eyes yellow
and rolling. Still we wanted to be given more.
So we told ourselves that love
was carried in the droopy looks it cast
from where it lay half-buried in the August dirt.

Why then—
sooner, later, always—did the turtle disappear?
We'd inspect the cage for leaks, find none,
But it was gone, and we'd fill a few summer weeks
mourning over the empty gray rubble
of hardware cloth. Until a new victim was found
to take the fugitive's place.

Then we grew up, gave up our little stalag.
My brother shaved his head and joined
a rock and roll band. And I—
how soon after?—moved away from home, began
taking lovers: strange men who appeared
in odd places, men who were skittish in the light.
Though at first they'd bristle
under my hands, with time their limbs grew trusting
uncoiling to reveal all the vulnerable

inner surfaces to my touch. I kept doors shut
so the house would fill with the thud of their big feet,
my voice pale at their heels:
Tell me I am lovely . . .
Tell me I'm not lonely . . .
Lovely?
Lonely?
Tell me, tell me . . .

I always wondered what made them run—
mornings I'd find my childhood losses come caving
back in on me: the tamed one's clothing
gone from the closet, no trace of his carcass,
not even a lone sock dropped on the lam.
And none have returned except in the shoes of
the next one who took his place.
Or maybe it was always the same man,
same turtle, who could tell the difference?
And armed with our half-belief in the hunt
as an endless cycle of capture and escape, escape
and capture, we gave each incumbent the same name:
Shank. Until the turtle
my brother found that last spring
while cleaning the cage for a new season of captives.
Its carapace was wedged under a rock, moldy
and flattened. Billiard pockets
where its limbs should have been when my brother turned
it over with a stick. Neither of us would pick it up.
And in that smelly, final darling
we saw there was no more use pretending
the looks they'd been giving us were those of a hunger
for anything we could provide.
Or that our love wasn't flawed and useless.
Or that we weren't just killing them with our care.

ᨠᨲ Gauntlet

The first time the blood came, after you left me,
I thought: well good, that's that—
at last assured you'd left no part of you behind
(I'd cut your books and photographs to ribbons).
But when the Rorschach spawning between my legs
dwindled to nothing, I mourned even that abandonment.
And every vacant window only mirrored your retreat—
the windbreaker huffing on your back as you fled down alleys
like a looter of shopwindows, a piece of me
tucked up into each armpit. I began to have regrets—
that I had not kept a tiny fist of cell and blood and tissue
inside me, something to wear your face in the moldy female dark—

not nostalgia, not romance, not grief: this diet of bread
and water, your wrists manacled like a French prisoner
to the wall of my belly, your cries muffling to liquid
as you drown in the womb's wet rags. Think
of the rat who serves as emblem after coups d'état
who is "introduced" (as though this were an affair
of high estate) into the vagina of a woman taken
as the spoils of war. (Were it not for the woman's suffering.)
Or maybe that need be here, too: maybe even the woman's suffering.
So think of the woman's suffering. And the rat's quavering
when he finds (the same as any rodent caught
in a field where three sides have just gone up in flame)
that his only way out is down the gauntlet of
the woman's cunt, the same way you've entered,
the same way you've stuck yourself here inside of me for good.

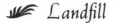 *Landfill*

for Margo and the rest of the old gang

The river was big water, and it swallowed me
the way it tried to swallow all the garbage they were driving
in, between the tracks and the river.
Bulldozers were forever pushing
humps of dirt into the greenish, muckish current,
shoring up the fill with clods of broken interstate.
Those humps became the home of rats

and idle girls, choking green on cigarettes,
come there to take the sacrament of pilfered wine.
As a bleary moon rose, she'd let the jeans drop from her waist,
clatter of glass from her hand and she dove,
naked, off the riprap. And I followed her
with clumsy strokes, into the September Hudson—
laying bets about which one of us would turn back first.

They say the river's poison now—
PCB. And you can walk further across it
than our skinny arms would ever carry us, without losing
dry ground. Today she's brought me back there,
transformed into a park where mothers bring their healthy kids
for civil, supervised play. The girls we were—
buried, with the freeway and the bottleglass, under a ballfield . . .

girls who swam until their courage failed, woke
with the filthy water lapping their hair and a pink sun rising
over Mecca. And though I know she had the better stroke,
the years made me believe she gave in first—
filling up her restless life with home and child, a child
who shrieks when I touch him, as though he knows
I'm still out treading in the wave-lap: my hand could drag him under.

She pats my hand as though I were her other child,
maybe showing me how sometimes turning back is moving on.
Then she loads her boy into a swing
and pushes him away, away
until his face becomes a blurring moon, blue eyes waxing
half in terror, half in the startled joy of freefall,
as he arcs the distance between here and those other days.

❧ Diptych: The Milk Carton Children

have been missing since last summer—
already their faces wear the slow
slurring of erasure, in the black-and-white
photographs screened beneath the wax hull
of this box where their absence is jailed:

Clarke "Toshira" Handa,

whose smudged face reveals just two
white features—a double row
of baby teeth and the sclera
of his eyes—who wears the same
striped jersey he wore the day
he was disappeared from Fairfield,
California: where the dead grass
would swallow his four-year-old height
and slaver him with August's tongue
. . . where even a crazyman's Chevy
would not be rusted through, idling
smooth while the boy at road's edge
drags his toe through a puddle of dust;

      and Antonella Mattina,

      whose hair and forehead erode
      in a mass of black dots, the rest
      of her white face hung in mid-smile,
      and—at twelve years old—in the middle
      of her season: her lips a dark bloom
      and her cheeks taking form, one resting
      against a blurred white shape—her hand,
      perhaps, but here resembling a curled
      length of bone washed from the Sound

to the shores of her native Long
Island, those stretches of mud
where a girl might find sea-glass,
strangers, the hollow bones of birds.

There is an address. A toll-free number
to call

if you can identify these children or any other
missing children please report any information
you may have . . .

But a bone, dead grass
and two black faces—
what does that signify?
And I see I've got no information
to report here, only fictions of a guilt
my own: that these words are not as empty
as my hands are empty, or that I won't
be soon delivering this sacred box
to the scatterings of midnight dogs
who'll nose the trash and drag its children
back into the same streets they were swallowed by.
And in the gray backwash of winter's leaving,
when the dogshit and the fruitrinds resurrect,
these faces too will rise, but bleached
so bad they're vacant, absent . . . gone,
just like the kids who wore those faces once.
Just like our short-lived vigil, kept
over those we helped the world consume.
And this despite our care and best intentions.

≈ Screamer

Who wasn't afraid of the damage/darkness might have crossed
    us with, in the guise of those loonies
who shared the house? The rest of the family tried swallowing
    its fear of each other—
we shut up and slept. Not you. All night your cries shot
    through my bedroom walls; by day
you left no clues that you'd been to the edge of that black pit
    in which the rest of us stood.
What did you see, looking down at us? We raised our bulbous
    fingers, straining
for gestures you read as the desperate grappling of those
    who would drag you in and choke you.
And then your eyes pitched in their sockets, lips dropping
    over your teeth as the mouth
ripped wide . . .

What came out were words gleaned from dark rock-and-rollers,
    the gutteral curses
issued from their black leather lips just before they spit
    on the audience, or worse:
Kill the mother! Kill and bring the old man down! Mascara
    ran their faces, free of tears.
But those nights had no stereo going, and the treble was up
    so loud the threats didn't sound human.
So we became a family well-armed with sleep, which was the
    sleep of Lethe, of forgetting.
We buried our heads in the pillows, father sang his own weekly
    rattling the bedsprings, and sometimes
I'd even catch the rush of mother's breathing—or was that you?
    Moaning? And we woke to cornflakes in the morning
without swerving.

*

Now, grown, you stand in daylight on my stoop, with a sensible
    trenchcoat against the rain,
reconciled to what manhood we gave you: shaving, the leather
    briefcase full of paper.
And the scream stretched tight around your skin, a membrane
    that can't be touched.
When I bring my body against yours in fumbling embrace, I find
    I don't know how to do it, where
I am allowed to put my hands. Up close your cheek is large,
    shapeless, too much like my own,
and I turn away, muttering my shamed avoidance of your eyes.
    Instead I put you on the sofa, give you tea—
now and then your saucer rattles; your narrow shoulders twitch
    and you give out a high, startled cry.
Then say *nothing, nothing.*

Brother, this is the howl I'd give you if it'd make me able
    to stay your lurching shoulders
with my hands. But any hands I ever had for you were
    meathooks—hooking you in and dragging you down
that welter of parents, siblings, scrambling over each other
    and choking out all the room
it takes to breathe. You fought your way out with your throat.
    But now, looking at you
wrestling your shoulders into place, I see you didn't escape
    unscarred, that no one escapes
being scarred at the hands of a man and woman who have a boy
    and want to bring him safely
across rough waters, to that farther shore where he will be
    A Man. No one makes it
without getting on his knees. Your famous rock-and-rollers
    tried, and mostly turned up dead,
and now it's you who goes on living.

✒ The Northside at Seven

Gray-sulphured light, having risen early this morning
in the west, over the stacks of Solvay, has by now
wafted across the lake and landed here on Lodi Street
where it anoints each particular with the general grace
of decay: the staggering rowhouses, the magazines flapping
from the gutters like broken skin, the red Dodge sedan
parked across the street from where I'm hunched in the pickup.
The Dodge's driver was ahead of me at the counter
in Ragusa's Bakery, making confession before an old woman
who was filling pastry shells with sweetened ricotta:

I put a new roof on her house, he was telling the woman,
but the lady don't pay me. I do a good job; she got no complaint.
But see, a man must hold his head high so I took her car.
The old woman trilled as she stuffed another log of cannoli.
To me, the man said, *She can call the cops if she wanna—*
I'll tell 'em I got kids to take care of, I gotta contract.
I shrugged: all the absolution I could bring myself to deliver
before grabbing the white paper sacks the woman slapped down
and walking out the door, leaving the man dropjawed and
unfinished in what he'd needed to tell me. I don't know;

there was something about his Sicilian features, his accent,
his whole goddamned hard-luck story that just gnawed on me so,
like those guys who came to unload on my own old man, muttering
Bobby, Bobby, see we got a little problem here Bobby . . .
the cue for women, kids to leave the room. But since then
my father has tried to draw me back into that room,
driving me along the tattered Bronx streets of his boyhood,
sometimes lifting his hands from the steering wheel and
spreading them, saying: *Look, these people are paysan,*
you're paysan, nothing you're ever gonna do can change that . . .

We'd spend the rest of the day on food, eating spiedini,
the anchovy sauce quenching what has become a chronic thirst
for salt, and shopping for the dense bread made from black
tailings of prosciutto, I forget the name of it now.
I forget so much. I even forget why tears come on the freeway,
mornings I drive by these old buildings when bread is cooking—
why? for what? Sometimes I feel history slipping from my body
like a guilty bone, the only way I have to call it back
is to sit here, slumped behind the wheel licking sugar from
my chin, right hand warmed by the semolina loaves riding shotgun,

the way my father might have spent his early mornings years ago,
before he claimed the responsibilities of manhood—of marrying
and making himself a daughter who would not be trapped, as he
felt he was, by streets washed over in the slow decay of light.
Making her different than he was. And making her the same.

Concerning Some Recent Theories of Physical Science

I have never questioned their Black Holes,
the proof of whose being requires no instrument
save the delicate sensors rigged under my skin
which tonight report no other signs of life.
This room is a vortex of infinite gravity:
it has the shape of your voice, but is empty,
and drags me toward my own implosion.
Tonight I am full of precarious atoms.

So don't think it hollow flattery that I ask
you to wear the robes of the next messiah:
I need you to save the universe.
To keep the night from collapsing into itself.
Outside, the spa's bronze Atlas is greasy with rain,
but like him you could stop the earth's tailspin
just by bringing here the naked muscles of your back.
And with your fingers you could save whole worlds.
If you came in this room now, I swear that space
would fill, our unwilling drift toward randomness
turned back the way of meaning and intent.
I could lay down science, lie down with you instead.

⚜ Firebomber

I wonder, sometimes, how they arrive: those children who
　　surface on the blank landscape
of dreams taking place in a train depot, or at a swimming pool,
　　their significant faces
yet a lapse of meaning—the gray-skinned boy from your high
　　school who had Cooley's anemia
and grew no more than four feet tall, the pigeon-toed redhead
　　who stole your sneakers
from the girl's locker room and wore them around on her slanting
　　feet, changing only the color
of the laces. I tell you *they* are the ones steering this busload
　　of circumstances we call:
A Life.

His name was Gary Zarrack, and what I remember most are the
　　spindly black hairs sprouting on his upper lip,
and that he was pudgy enough to have small breasts whose
　　nipples saluted the salt wind
as he stood on the float that rocked maybe fifteen yards out
　　in the Hudson.
My mother brought me to swim in the river, not seeming to care
　　that the water left
mysterious brown patches on my thighs. As I pedalled my timid
　　wrists under my chin,
she kicked away sand from the base of the riprap forming a wall
　　behind the beach,
in search of paleozoic flowers. And she always found them—
　　papery stems through the granite,
fossilized. I might have been drowning—swimming, which I had
　　not yet mastered, churning my way
toward that boy on the float.

Other kids from my neighborhood were not allowed to swim
　　there. Their mothers

had them swim between tiles, learn patterns of china, the spell
    of infectious disease:
Typhoid. Meningitis.
But my mother didn't look when I caught a thick mouthful of
    water and came up sputtering,
and I remember peeing through the bottom of my suit on a rock
    that I picked up after,
to see how it smelled. When I questioned her shoulder, her eyes
    fixed on the far shore,
as though it were futile trying to explain me the difference
    between *jurassic* and *triassic.*
No other grownups patrolled the river's children, who were dark
    and whose names had many vowels.
Guineas, they called themselves. And the freckled ones: *Micks.*
    Wednesday afternoons
I sat beside them at catechism, my body stoppered with fear
    as it glinted like sand
from the black iris of a nun's eye. I didn't belong—
after church on Sundays, I'd go down to the dirty storefronts
    with my father
for jawbreakers and his copy of *The New York Times.* Sometimes
    he'd let drop the holy word *attorney*
and the whole drugstore would go dead: Depaoli the garbage-
    man, and Joe Albanese
whose hands shuffled heroes in the deli . . . and Carmela
    Mannino, who stopped traffic
when we crossed the street after catechism, her feet monstrous
    slabs in the red platform shoes
she wore to stand above the hoods of cars. They never said a
    word. And I sensed that silence
when I swam with their sons, their daughters, down in the river,
    kids who bullied
Good-Humors out of smaller children's hands, who threw stones
    that whistled behind my mother's back
when she wasn't looking. When I finally reached the white float

after what seemed like an hour
flailing against my body's desire to be buried in the green water,
    the boy would look
down the top of my suit as I struggled to hoist up, then poke
    menacingly, with his foot,
at what my mother taught me to call *my bosom*. Too frightened
    to cry at the pain,
I was also tingling—from a warm place below my skin, unleashed
    when he asked:
ya got a cigratt on ya, punk-o, by any chance?

He must have been in ninth grade when he threw a Coca-Cola
    bottle full of gasoline into the stone church,
splattering the big window with Mary holding a skinny & slashed-
    up Jesus on her knee,
and even though it was right out on the only two-lane road in
    town, the church went up like magnesium;
by the time the volunteer firetruck got there, flames were licking
    all the windows, and—*magic!*—
everything inside was gone, the plaster stations of the cross
    vaporized without a trace,
and the rows of veiled women singing *Ave Maria* to a flesh-colored
    guy on a stick/now just
forty charred bolts on a flourful of ash.

They made do, holding mass in the parochial school's gymnasium.
In a way, the firebombing seemed a tremendous gift:
like the old wooden altar, the ancient priests were lost
    to their own decay—
long-haired Jesuits appeared with slides of burning Asian babies,
    tapes of Simon & Garfunkel;
everyone sat on tumbling mats on the floor, drinking dixie
    cups of cheap wine
and eating the crackers of Christ's body, afterward shaking hands,
    saying *Peace Be With You.*
But the young priests left us for the arms of women, and left us

to slackjawed monsignors
who set up folding chairs in the gym and sent around a copper
    plate for a new church.
Not for refugees this time.

The war ended anyway. Even though the masonry still stood
    as though the fire never happened
they built that new church: low white brick with plate glass
    sliding doors and one stained glass panel—
an indecipherable collage of shards. Every month they'd bring
    a troop of well-scrubbed teenagers
in yellow suits and dresses, to play guitars and sing *Kum-bay-ya*.
    But it wasn't the same:
no candles glowing in the dark from small pots of colored glass,
    no sepia-faced virgins on the window,
the garments painted to hint at Mary's secular, porcelain knees,
    lurking below the red velvet.
I don't know who went to church after that: bleached widows
    in sheared-fox coats, maybe,
but no old *tias* cuffing young boys afterwards on the steps,
    cursing in Italian.
My father had the Sunday paper delivered to the house, and we
    stopped going to mass,
though my mother disappeared wordlessly every Sunday for an
    hour.
One day a negro man my mother hired to clean the yard hauled
    away a heap of old stones he found—
when my mother realized what he'd done, she said it was all right,
    forget it, it didn't matter anymore.
That summer Tommy O'Neill fell attempting a high-dive off the
    crane down at the docks, missed the river
and busted open his skull on the riprap. My mother stopped
    taking me swimming: the danger, sure—
or maybe she'd just lost interest.

I never found out how they knew it was Gary Zarrack who'd set
    fire to the old church, and he too
disappeared. I saw him though, a year or more later, in the hall
    of the high school.
He was taller, and thinner, surrounded by a huddle of skinny
    girls in chipped nail polish
who cooed and rubbed against him. He was wearing a starched
    green uniform with a lot of gold braid—
on top of his buzz-cut a peaked cap that divided his head like
    the pitch of a roof
and dipped over his forehead, nearly to his eye. He swaggered
    while the girls clucked over his metal,
then looked up and saw me: I am sure he did not remember who
    I was.
But I raised my hands, palms toward him—and I let them hang
    in the air that way.
My Haunting Stranger: I wanted him to know how he'd changed
    me with his hands, that night
he came to stand before the glowing windows, how one small
    release in the wrist was all it took
to send the blue glass arcing across the night, a rush of fire
    at the Virgin's mouth
and then us waking, as though from a vivid dream, to find cold
    air invading our bedrooms
while we slept.

🌾 Photojournalism

—On the 20th anniversary of the Tet offensive

The face is now famous:
an Asian man, just more than a boy, whose eyes are clenched,
his teeth braced & showing one last bark or cry
caught visibly in back his throat.
The executioner's face is turned away
from the frame, so that all we see is his arm, and his pistol,
which is, inherently, a dead thing, and therefore morally
exempt, neutral, the one fact in the picture.
Like an apostrophe tacked to a word, what it does is
establish possession, without itself signifying.

And not far away, maybe just a few feet, another man
stands with a 35-mm camera and likewise points and shoots.
His pact made long ago: not
to hurl his shoulder into the gut of the man who'll kill,
nor to cry out for god (or, more courageously, man)
to stop the bullet's traverse through its intended skull.
Instead, he allows this to be done.
And the lens becomes another neutral fact of the picture,
not an eye but a mouth, a mouth with teeth,
inside of which the world gets chewed to pulp.
And those who stand behind the camera and the gun
are both the same in this regard: men who see the world
the way our unintruding god must see it
—as being full of their own children—
and they eat their children to keep the rest of us strong.

✐ Field Guide to the Dead & Dying Flowers of Eastern North America

September's the best time for learning the mechanisms of rot:
    the soft parts go first.
And you go running—down the right-of-way of the abandoned
    Utica-Mohawk Line.
The teasel has dried into spears that line the railroad embankment
    like combat police standing guard
in a smoldered, demilitarized land. And the soft herbs of June
    have transformed into concertina,
snarls barricading a ghetto where the summer's last stragglers
    eke out the slow thread of their dying.
You enter with caution, each stalk a foreboding—: starved
    like the bone in a holocaust shin.

But sure, there's still flowers. Deep in the rabbly tangles,
    if you slowed and dropped
onto knees and hands, you'd find mallow, evening primrose—
    you've seen the tell-tale glitter
of a pink too sharp for the dying, a green kept moist in the
    shade. If you crawled through prickerbushes
and down the embankment, you'd come to the edge of a slough
    full of oil-rainbowed water
where goldenrod blooms in the height of its season, and asters
    and touch-me-not and even Sweet
Joe-Pye-Weed/fill the bellies of old Maytags that people
    have torched on the banks,

which is also where they found her—two weeks past, maybe
    three—her body tossed to the claws
of the Great Burdock, where she wrestled like a dancing doll
    while her stabwounds
bled into the oily ground. You did not see her come, nor go,
    but for a few days running
you could've sworn you smelled meat along one stretch of tracks.

A week of sun and her bones rose,
her skin turning to parchment, the jackknife stuck in her throat
    still standing
long after wild dogs and skunks had come in the night to haul
    her soft parts away.

To find her, it took two boys
hunting frogs with those wide, sharp-pointed forks.
Police came and photographed the rebus of her bones.
And afterwards, you went down there
to study the spots where the weeds were matted.
It was interesting, and you were surprised
at how you weren't afraid.

Now even friends turn parental, warning you never to run there
    alone because the brush is thick with evil.
But still you come home at dusk, skin greased like an Arab bride,
    and your man trains his Clark Kent
miracle eyes on the sweaty clothes puddling around your feet,
    your persistence a thorn.
Today you ran panicked toward what looked like a spotfire
    ahead; closer, and you saw it was a bright hawkweed
that had fought its way up through two feet of gravel to blossom.
    Astonishing, how such a thing endures.
As you intend enduring, keeping what few secrets lie inside of
    you inside of you: heroic myths, ugly rumors—
about God and about some ancient rites of spring.

❧ Dangerous Life

I quit med school when I found out the stiff they gave me
had Book Nine of *Paradise Lost* and the lyrics
to "Louie, Louie" tattooed on the inside of her thighs.

That morning as the wind was mowing
little ladies on a street below, I touched a bunsen burner
to the Girlscout sash whose badges were the measure of my worth:

Careers . . .
Cookery, Seamstress . . .
and *Baby Maker* . . . all gone up in smoke.

But I kept the merit badge marked *Dangerous Life*,
for which, if you remember, the girls were taken to the woods
and taught the mechanics of fire,

around which they had us dance with pointed sticks
lashed into crucifixes that we'd wrapped with yarn and wore
on lanyards round our necks, calling them "The Eyes of God."

Now my mother calls the payphone outside my walk-up, raving
about what people think of a woman: thirty, unsettled,
living on foodstamps, coin op laundromats & public clinics.

Some nights I take my lanyards from their shoebox, practice baying
those old campsongs to the moon. And remember how they told us
that a smart girl could find her way out of anywhere, alive.

❧ The Revelation

I hit Tonapah at sunset,
just when the billboards advertising the legal brothels
turn dun-colored as the sun lies
down behind the strip mine.

I found all the whores of Babylon
in the Safeway, buying frozen foods
and cokes for the sitter before their evening shifts.
Yes they gave excuses to cut
ahead of me in line, probably wrote bad checks,
but still they were lovely at that hour,
their hair newly washed
and ravelling. If you follow
any one of the apparitions far enough—
the fallen ones: idolaters, the thieves
and liars—you will find that beauty, a cataclysmic
beauty rising off the face of a burning landscape
just before the appearance of the beast, the beauty
that is the flower of our dying into another life.
Like a Möbius strip: you go round once
and you come out on the other side.
There is no alpha, no omega,
no beginning and no end.
Only the ceaseless swell
and fall of sunlight on those rusted hills.
Watch the way brilliance turns
on darkness. How can any of us be damned.

A NOTE ON THE POET

Lucia Maria Perillo was born in New York City in 1958. For a number of years she worked for the U.S. Fish and Wildlife Service and the National Park Service. She attended Syracuse University's Creative Writing Program and now teaches at Saint Martin's College in Olympia, Washington.

A NOTE ON THE PRIZE

The Samuel French Morse Poetry Prize was established in 1983 by the Northeastern University Department of English in order to honor Professor Morse's distinguished career as teacher, scholar, and poet. The members of the prize committee are Francis C. Blessington, Joseph deRoche, Victor Howes, Stuart Peterfreund, and Guy Rotella.